GREAT GRILLING
AND MORE
ALDI® RECIPES FOR *Thrilling GRILLING*

Visit us at
www.ALDI.com

Distributed by ALDI® Inc.
Batavia, IL 60510-1477

Some of the products listed in this publication may be in limited distribution or only available seasonally.

Photography on pages 7 and 11 by Chris Cassidy Photography, Inc.

Ingredient photography by Shaughnessy MacDonald, Inc.

Pictured on the front cover *(top to bottom):* Backyard Barbecue Burger *(page 18)* and Tuscan Garden BBQ Steaks *(page 12).*

Pictured on the back cover *(clockwise from top):* Thai Grilled Chicken *(page 38),* Garlic Skewered Shrimp *(page 62)* and Spicy Ribs *(page 22).*

ISBN-13: 978-1-4127-2423-4
ISBN-10: 1-4127-2423-6

Manufactured in U.S.A.

8 7 6 5 4 3 2 1

Microwave Cooking: Microwave ovens vary in wattage. Use the cooking times as guidelines and check for doneness before adding more time.

Table of Contents

ALDI® specializes in a select assortment of high-quality, private label products at the lowest possible prices. Quality, taste and satisfaction are always DOUBLE* guaranteed at **ALDI®**. We're so confident about the quality of our products we guarantee you'll be satisfied too!

*Excludes non-food special purchase items and alcohol.

Nothing beats the flavor of food hot off the grill! Whether you're preparing a weeknight meal for the family, hosting a weekend party or planning a family reunion, **ALDI**® has a full choice of delicious, affordable foods for every grilling occasion. Start with the perfect main dish—top quality beef, pork, poultry or fish. Then, round out the meal with flavorful appetizers, crunchy snacks, fresh salads, refreshing summer drinks and fun desserts.

Is it done yet?

The grilling times for meat, poultry and fish may be different from their conventional cooking times. The following tips and guidelines will help insure delicious grilled foods that are cooked to a safe internal temperature.

USDA* Recommended Grilling Times (4 inches from heat source)		
Beef		
¾ inch thick	Steaks	8 to 10 minutes
Pork		
¾ inch thick	Pork Loin Chops	6 to 8 minutes
½ to 1½ pounds	Pork Tenderloins	15 to 20 minutes
2 to 4 pounds	Ribs (indirect heat)	1½ to 2 hours
Chicken		
4 ounces	Drumsticks and Wings	16 to 24 minutes
4 to 8 ounces	Leg Quarters	20 to 30 minutes
4 ounces	Boneless Breasts	12 to 16 minutes
3 to 5 pounds	Whole Chickens	1 to 1½ hours
Fish (FDA** recommended grilling time)		
	10 minutes per inch of thickness	

Instant-Read Thermometer

An instant-read thermometer is one of the most important cooking tools you own. Use the chart on *page 5* as a temperature guide.

Watch foods carefully during grilling. Total cooking time will vary with the type of food, position on the grill, weather, temperature of the heat and the degree of doneness you desire. Not everyone judges the temperature of the grill exactly alike. The time ranges in our recipes are recommendations. For perfectly done food, use our times as guides and watch all foods on the grill closely. Use an instant-read thermometer to test for doneness whenever possible.

Meat and Fish Doneness Tips

Beef

The safe temperature for medium-rare steaks is 145°F. Larger cuts can be removed from the grill and allowed to stand, covered, for 10 to 15 minutes. The temperature will continue to rise 5°F to 10°F degrees. The juices will redistribute throughout the meat during this time.

To judge doneness visually, make a small cut near the bone, or near the center for boneless cuts. Medium-rare will be very pink in the inside center and slightly brown toward the exterior. Medium steak will be light pink in the center and brown toward the exterior.

Pork

All pork cuts should be grilled to 160°F. Cuts like pork tenderloin can be removed from the grill at 150°F or 155°F and allowed to stand, covered, until the temperature rises to 160°F. Grilled and smoked pork can often remain pink even when well done. It's best to rely on an instant-read thermometer to determine doneness.

Fish

Fish should be cooked to 145°F. A marinade or sauce keeps fish moist during grilling. Fish and shellfish are fully cooked when the color turns from translucent to opaque (usually white). Fish is done when it just begins to flake when tested with a fork.

Burger Doneness

If you think you can tell visually that a burger has been cooked to a safe temperature, think again. According to the USDA*, one out of every four burgers turns brown in the middle before it has reached a safe internal temperature (and some burgers that are pink inside are perfectly safe!).

Pick up the patty with tongs and insert an instant-read thermometer into the center of the patty. The temperatures should reach 160°F for beef burgers and 165°F for ground turkey burgers.

The Mystery of Marinades

A marinade—a seasoned liquid mixture or vinaigrette—is used to add flavor and sometimes to tenderize meat. Marinades also help to keep food moist.

Flavoring Marinades

A flavoring marinade is used with tender cuts of meat, such as T-bone, rib eye, strip or sirloin steaks, pork chops and chicken breasts, for a short time—15 minutes to 2 hours.

Tenderizing Marinades

A tenderizing marinade contains a food acid or a tenderizing enzyme such as lemon or lime juice, vinegar, Italian dressing, yogurt, salsa or wine. Less tender cuts should be marinated at least 6 hours, but no more than 24 hours. Food marinated for longer than 24 hours will have a mushy texture.

Marinate Safely

Many grilling recipes call for marinating meat to boost flavor. Make sure the marinade used doesn't boost bacteria counts, too. If you want to baste meat with the marinade during grilling or serve it as a sauce, the safest practice is to set aside some of the marinade ahead of time. Discard the marinade that was used to marinate the uncooked meat. Use the reserved portion for basting or serve it as a sauce.

Direct and Indirect Grilling

Direct heat is used for smaller and thinner pieces of food such as steaks, chops, chicken breasts, kabobs and fish. Place food directly over the coals or fire.

Indirect heat is for larger cuts of meat and poultry such as roasts, whole chickens and ribs. These cuts need to cook over low heat for a longer time. To cook with indirect heat, place the food directly over a drip pan with the coals around the pan, or for gas grills with 2 burners, place the food over the burner that is turned off.

Sizzling Good Grilling

ALDI® is pleased to share with you a terrific selection of sizzling good recipes. Shop your local **ALDI®** store (www.aldi.com) to save big on important ingredients found in these recipes. With Incredible Value Every Day, you'll find only top-quality products for great grilling and affordable meals all year long.

Grill to a Safe Internal Temperature
USDA* Safe Internal Temperatures for Meat

Beef		
Ground Beef		160°F
Steaks		
	Medium Rare	145°F
	Medium	160°F
	Well Done	170°F
Pork		
Chops and Tenderloin		
	Medium	160°F
	Well Done	170°F
Poultry		
Ground Chicken and Turkey		165°F
Chicken Breasts		170°F
Chicken Thighs, Wings and Legs		180°F
Whole Chicken		180°F
Fish		
The FDA** suggests cooking fish to an internal temperature of 145°F.		

*USDA is the United States Department of Agriculture, which regulates all meats and poultry.

**FDA is the U.S. Food and Drug Administration, which regulates all fish and seafood.

Granger® Great Grilled Beef

CHAPTER 1

Granger® T-Bone Steaks with Grilled Mushrooms

¼ **cup Carlini® olive oil**
2 **tablespoons Spice Club® minced garlic**
1 **teaspoon Spice Club® black pepper**
½ **teaspoon dried thyme**
1 **package (8 ounces) fresh mushrooms, cleaned and stems trimmed**
4 **Granger® T-bone steaks, thawed**
Sebree® salt

1. If using wooden skewers, soak 4 skewers in water 30 minutes. Combine oil, garlic, pepper and thyme in small bowl; set aside. Spray cold grid of grill with Ariel® no stick cooking spray. Prepare grill for direct cooking.

2. Thread mushrooms on skewers. Brush mushrooms and steaks with oil mixture. Place on grid over medium-hot heat. Grill, covered, 8 to 10 minutes or until desired doneness, turning steaks and mushrooms occasionally. Brush mushrooms with remaining oil mixture up to last 5 minutes of cooking. Season mushrooms with salt before serving.

Makes 4 servings

Grilled Beef Salad

4 Granger® Cajun- or teriyaki-flavored flat iron grillers
½ cup Burman's® mayonnaise
2 tablespoons Happy Harvest® white vinegar
1 tablespoon Briargate® spicy brown mustard
½ teaspoon Sweet Harvest® sugar
½ teaspoon Spice Club® roasted minced garlic
6 cups Freshire Farms® garden salad, torn into pieces
2 large tomatoes, seeded and chopped
⅓ cup chopped fresh basil (optional)
2 slices red onion, separated into rings
½ cup Chef's Cupboard® cheese and garlic croutons
Spice Club® black pepper (optional)

1. Thaw steaks according to package directions. Combine mayonnaise, vinegar, mustard, sugar and garlic in small bowl; mix well. Cover; refrigerate until serving. Toss together lettuce, tomatoes, basil and onion in large bowl. Cover; refrigerate until serving.

2. Spray cold grid of grill with Ariel® no stick cooking spray. Prepare grill for direct cooking. Place steaks on grid over medium heat. Grill, covered, 6 to 8 minutes or until desired doneness, turning once. Transfer steaks to carving board. Slice each in half lengthwise; carve crosswise into thin slices.

3. Add steak and croutons to lettuce mixture; toss well. Add mayonnaise mixture; toss to coat. Serve with additional black pepper.

Makes 4 servings

Meal Idea
Complete your meal with Buehler's® Jumbo Biscuits, iced tea made from Benner® instant tea and the Snackin' Banana Split on page 90.

Rib Eye Steaks with Chili Butter

½ cup (1 stick) Happy Farms® butter, softened
2 teaspoons chili powder
1 teaspoon Spice Club® minced garlic in olive oil
1 teaspoon Briargate® Dijon mustard
⅛ teaspoon ground red pepper or chipotle chili pepper
4 Granger® beef rib eye steaks, thawed
1 teaspoon Spice Club® black pepper

1. Combine butter, chili powder, garlic, mustard and red pepper in small bowl. Beat until smooth. Place butter mixture on sheet of waxed paper. Using waxed paper, roll mixture back and forth into 6-inch log. (If butter is too soft, refrigerate up to 30 minutes. Reroll to form log.) Wrap waxed paper around butter log to seal. Refrigerate at least 1 hour or up to 2 days.

2. Spray cold grid of grill with Ariel® no stick cooking spray. Prepare grill for direct cooking.

3. Rub black pepper evenly over steaks. Place on grid over medium-hot heat. Grill, covered, 8 to 10 minutes or until desired doneness, turning occasionally.

4. Served grilled steaks with slices of Chili Butter.

Makes 4 servings

Serve with Grilled Garlic Bread

Slice L'oven Fresh® garlic bread. Place, cut sides down, on the grid about 2 minutes before the end of cooking time. Grill until lightly toasted. Serve immediately.

Tuscan Garden BBQ Steaks

4 Granger® New York strip loin steaks

1 bottle (12 ounces) Tuscan Garden lemon pepper or garden herb marinade

1 teaspoon cracked black pepper *or* ½ teaspoon Spice Club® black pepper

Sebree® salt

1. Place steaks in Kwik-N-Fresh® gallon freezer bag or 11×17-inch baking dish. Add marinade. Seal bag; turn to coat steaks with marinade. Marinate in refrigerator 2 to 8 hours.

2. Spray cold grid of grill with Ariel® no stick cooking spray. Prepare grill for direct cooking. Remove steaks from marinade; discard bag and marinade. Rub pepper over surface of steaks.

3. Place steaks on grid over medium heat. Grill, covered, 10 to 12 minutes or until desired doneness, turning occasionally. Season with salt before serving.

Makes 4 servings

Beef and Pineapple Kabobs

1 boneless beef sirloin steak
1 small onion, finely chopped
½ cup teriyaki sauce
1 can (20 ounces) Sweet Harvest® chunk pineapple, drained
1 can (8 ounces) whole water chestnuts, drained

1. Spray cold grid of grill with Ariel® no stick cooking spray. Prepare grill for direct cooking. Cut steak into ¼-inch-thick strips. For marinade, combine onion and teriyaki sauce in small bowl. Add beef strips, stirring to coat.

2. If using wooden skewers, soak in water for 30 minutes. Alternately thread beef strips (weaving back and forth), pineapple chunks and water chestnuts onto skewers. Place kabobs on grid over medium heat. Grill, covered, 4 to 6 minutes turning once or until desired doneness. Serve immediately. *Makes 4 servings*

Grilling Lesson: Use flat skewers to keep the chunks from slipping around when you turn the kabobs.

Fajitas with Avocado Salsa

4 B-Bar® filet of sirloin steaks, thawed
¼ cup Northstar® light beer, or tequila (optional)
3 tablespoons fresh lime juice
1 tablespoon minced La Mas Rica® jalapeño peppers
1 teaspoon Spice Club® minced garlic in olive oil
Avocado Salsa (page 15)
8 La Mas Rica® flour or corn tortillas
1 large red bell pepper, cut lengthwise into 4 pieces
1 large green bell pepper, cut lengthwise into 4 pieces
4 slices red onion, cut ½ inch thick

1. Place steaks in Kwik-N-Fresh® gallon freezer bag. Combine beer, lime juice, jalapeño and garlic in small bowl; pour over steaks. Seal bag; turn to coat. Marinate in refrigerator 1 to 4 hours, turning once.

2. Prepare Avocado Salsa.

3. Coat cold grid of grill with Carlini® vegetable oil. Prepare grill for direct cooking. Wrap tortillas in Kwik-N-Fresh® aluminum foil.

4. Remove steaks from bag; discard bag and marinade. Place steaks, bell peppers and onion slices on grid over medium heat. Grill, covered, 8 to 10 minutes for medium-rare to medium or until desired doneness. Turn steaks, bell peppers and onion slices halfway through grilling time. Place tortilla packet on grid during last 5 to 7 minutes of grilling; turn halfway through grilling time to heat through.

5. Transfer steaks to cutting board. Cut across the grain into thin slices. Slice bell peppers into thin strips. Separate onion slices into rings. Equally divide peppers, onions and Avocado Salsa among tortillas. Roll up and serve.

Makes 4 servings

Avocado Salsa

1 large ripe avocado, diced
1 large tomato, seeded and diced
3 tablespoons chopped fresh cilantro
1 tablespoon Carlini® vegetable oil
1 tablespoon fresh lime juice
2 teaspoons minced La Mas Rica® jalapeño peppers
½ teaspoon Spice Club® minced garlic in olive oil
½ teaspoon Sebree® salt

Place avocado in medium bowl. Gently stir in tomato, cilantro, oil, lime juice, jalapeño, garlic and salt until well combined. Let stand at room temperature while grilling steak. Cover and refrigerate if preparing in advance. Bring to room temperature before serving.   *Makes about 1½ cups*

Skewered Beef Strips with Teriyaki Honey Glaze

4 B-Bar® beef filet of sirloin steaks, partially thawed
1 bottle (12 ounces) Tuscan Garden teriyaki-flavored marinade, divided
⅓ cup Golden Nectar® honey

1. Slice steaks into ¼-inch-thick strips. If using wooden skewers, soak in water 30 minutes. Thread beef strips onto 12 skewers and place in large glass baking dish. Pour ½ cup marinade over strips. Cover; marinate 10 minutes, turning once.

2. Spray cold grid of grill with Ariel® no stick cooking spray. Prepare grill for direct cooking.

3. Combine honey and ¼ cup marinade. Remove skewers from marinade; discard marinade. Brush honey glaze over beef.

4. Grill skewers 3 to 4 minutes. Boil remaining honey glaze 3 minutes. Serve as dipping sauce. *Makes 4 servings*

Cooking Lesson: To easily cut even strips, partially thaw frozen steaks before slicing. If using fresh steaks, partially freeze before slicing.

Teriyaki Honey Glazed Pork

Try Teriyaki Honey Glaze with Roseland® center cut pork chops. Brush the glaze on the chops during the last 5 minutes of cooking. Be sure to make extra honey glaze for a dipping sauce.

Teriyaki Honey Glazed Chicken

Cut Kirkland® chicken tenders or breasts into long strips. Thread strips onto skewers. Marinate 10 minutes in Teriyaki Honey Glaze. Grill skewers 6 to 8 minutes, brushing with marinade and turning frequently. Be sure to make extra honey glaze for a dipping sauce.

Backyard Barbecue Burgers

1½ pounds ground beef or ground sirloin
⅓ cup Briargate® Kansas City-style BBQ sauce, divided
1 to 2 tomatoes, cut into thick slices
1 onion, cut into thick slices
1 to 2 tablespoons Carlini® olive oil
6 L'oven Fresh® hamburger buns
Green or red leaf lettuce

1. Spray cold grid of grill with Ariel® cooking spray. Prepare grill for direct cooking. Combine beef and 2 tablespoons barbecue sauce in large bowl. Shape into six 1-inch-thick patties.

2. Place patties on grid over medium heat. Grill, covered, 8 to 10 minutes (or, uncovered, 13 to 15 minutes) to medium (160°F) or until desired doneness, turning occasionally and brushing with BBQ sauce.

3. Meanwhile, brush tomato and onion slices* with oil. Place on grid. Grill tomato slices 2 to 3 minutes and onion slices about 10 minutes. Just before serving, place buns, cut side down, on grid; grill until lightly toasted. Serve patties on rolls with tomatoes, onions and lettuce. *Makes 6 servings*

*Onion slices may be cooked in 2 tablespoons oil in large skillet over medium heat 10 minutes until tender and slightly brown.

Mexicali Burgers

Guacamole (recipe follows)
1 pound ground beef or ground sirloin
⅓ cup crushed Casa Mamita® nacho tortilla chips
⅓ cup prepared Casa Mamita® salsa
3 tablespoons finely chopped fresh cilantro (optional)
2 tablespoons finely chopped onion
1 teaspoon ground cumin
4 slices Happy Farms® deli sliced Pepper Jack or Cheddar cheese
4 L'oven Fresh® hamburger buns
Lettuce leaves
Sliced tomatoes
Casa Mamita® white round tortilla chips

1. Prepare Guacamole. Spray cold grid of grill with Ariel® no stick cooking spray. Prepare grill for direct cooking.

2. Combine beef, nacho tortilla chips, salsa, cilantro, onion and cumin in medium bowl until well blended. Shape mixture into 4 patties. Place patties on grid over medium heat. Grill, covered, 8 to 10 minutes (or, uncovered, 13 to 15 minutes) to medium (160°F) or until desired doneness, turning once.

3. Place 1 slice cheese on each burger during last 1 to 2 minutes of grilling. If desired, place rolls, cut side down, on grill to toast lightly during last 1 to 2 minutes of grilling. Serve burgers on buns with Guacamole, lettuce, tomatoes and white tortilla chips.

Makes 4 servings

Guacamole

1 ripe avocado, pitted
1 tablespoon Casa Mamita® salsa
1 teaspoon lime or lemon juice
¼ teaspoon Spice Club® garlic powder
¼ teaspoon Sebree® salt

Place avocado in medium bowl; mash with fork until avocado is slightly chunky. Add salsa, lime juice, garlic powder and salt; blend well. *Makes about ½ cup*

Roseland® Backyard Pork & Ribs

CHAPTER 2

Spicy Ribs

2 tablespoons Carlini® olive oil
2 slabs (about 4 to 6 pounds) pork spareribs
½ cup packed Sweet Harvest® brown sugar
4 teaspoons dry mustard
4 teaspoons Spice Club® seasoned salt
2 teaspoons Spice Club® garlic powder
2 teaspoons Spice Club® black pepper
⅔ to 1 cup Briargate® barbecue sauce
½ teaspoon Kahlner's® red pepper or jalapeño sauce

1. Prepare grill for *indirect* cooking. Pour 1 tablespoon olive oil over each slab of ribs; rub to coat. Combine brown sugar, mustard, seasoned salt, garlic powder and pepper in small bowl. Rub mixture evenly over ribs.

2. Place ribs on grid directly over drip pan. Grill, covered, over medium heat 1 hour, turning occasionally.

3. Meanwhile, combine barbecue sauce and pepper sauce in small bowl. Baste ribs generously with sauce; grill 30 minutes more or until ribs are tender, turning and basting with sauce occasionally. Bring any remaining sauce mixture to a boil over medium-high heat; boil 1 minute. Serve ribs with remaining sauce. *Makes 4 servings*

Tex-Mex Pork Kabobs
with Chili Sour Cream Sauce

1 cup Friendly Farms sour cream
¾ teaspoon cumin
¾ teaspoon chili powder
¼ teaspoon Sebree® salt
¼ teaspoon Spice Club® garlic powder
¼ teaspoon onion powder
¼ teaspoon oregano
2 Appleton® peppercorn-flavored pork tenderloins, cut into 1½-inch pieces
1 large yellow bell pepper, cored, seeded and cut into small chunks
1 large red bell pepper, cored, seeded and cut into small chunks
1 large green bell pepper, cored, seeded and cut into small chunks

1. Combine sour cream, cumin, chili powder, salt, garlic powder, onion powder and oregano in small bowl; mix well. Cover; refrigerate 2 to 3 hours.

2. If using wooden skewers, soak in water 30 minutes before using. Spray cold grid of grill with Ariel® no stick cooking spray. Prepare grill for direct cooking.

3. Thread meat and peppers onto 6 skewers. Grill, covered, over medium-hot heat 10 to 12 minutes or until desired doneness, turning several times. Serve immediately with sour cream sauce.

Makes 4 to 6 servings

Grilling Lesson

Use tongs or a spatula, instead of a fork, to turn meats. Flavorful juices are lost when meats are pieced with a fork.

Appleton® Grilled Pork Tenderloin Medallions

1 to 2 Appleton® peppercorn-flavored pork tenderloins
1 tablespoon dried basil
1 tablespoon dried thyme
1½ teaspoons dried rosemary
1 teaspoon paprika
  Carlini® olive oil

1. Slice tenderloin into 8 to 10 medallions; set aside. Combine basil, thyme, rosemary and paprika in Kwik-N-Fresh® gallon freezer bag.

2. Spray cold grid of grill with Ariel® no stick cooking spray. Prepare grill for direct cooking.

3. Brush medallions with olive oil. Add medallions to bag; shake to coat. Place pork on grid over medium-hot heat. Grill, covered, 4 to 5 minutes per side or until desired doneness.

Makes 4 to 6 servings

Meal Idea

Appleton® marinated pork tenderloins are excellent for any grilling occasion. Whether you're hosting a party or preparing a last-minute patio dinner, everyone will rave about the terrific flavor. Just add a salad and grilled vegetables. Dinner will be on the table under 30 minutes. And, be sure to grill extra tenderloins for sandwiches and salads later in the week.

Barbecued Pork Tenderloin Sandwiches

1 cup Kyder® tomato ketchup
½ cup packed Sweet Harvest® brown sugar
½ teaspoon dry mustard
½ teaspoon ground red pepper
2 Appleton® teriyaki-flavored pork tenderloins
1 large red onion, cut into ½-inch-thick slices
6 hoagie or sandwich rolls

1. Combine ketchup, brown sugar, mustard and red pepper in small saucepan; mix well. Bring to a boil over medium-high heat. Reduce heat to low; simmer, uncovered, 5 to 8 minutes or until thickened, stirring occasionally. Set aside half of sauce.

2. Spray cold grid of grill with Ariel® no stick cooking spray. Prepare grill for direct cooking. Place tenderloins on center of grid over medium-hot heat. Grill, covered, 10 minutes, turning once. Place onion slices on grid. Brush tenderloins and onions with sauce. Grill onions 8 to 10 minutes or until soft. Do not turn. Continue to grill pork, covered, 5 to 15 minutes or until internal temperature reaches 155°F when tested with meat thermometer inserted lengthwise into tenderloins.

3. Transfer tenderloins and onions to cutting board; tent with Kwik-N-Fresh® aluminum foil. Let stand 10 to 15 minutes before carving. Internal temperature will continue to rise 5°F to 10°F during stand time. Carve tenderloins crosswise into thin slices. Separate onion slices into rings. Divide pork and onion rings among rolls; drizzle with reserved sauce.

Makes 6 servings

Grilling Lesson

Grilling food over too high heat can char the outside before the center has a chance to reach the desired doneness. The most accurate way to determine doneness is with an instant-read thermometer (pictured on page 4), inserted horizontally from the side into the center. Be sure to cover the indentation on the stem to ensure the thermometer will accurately measure the temperature. Do not leave an instant-read thermometer in the meat during grilling since these thermometers are not heat proof.

Grilled Pork and Potatoes Vesuvio

1½ pounds small red potatoes (about 1½ inches in diameter), scrubbed
2 teaspoons Spice Club® minced garlic in olive oil, divided
1 teaspoon Carlini® olive oil
Sebree® salt
Spice Club® black pepper
1 to 2 Appleton® peppercorn-flavored pork tenderloins
6 lemon wedges
¼ cup chopped fresh Italian or curly leaf parsley
1 teaspoon finely grated lemon peel

1. Place potatoes in single layer in microwavable dish. Pierce each potato with tip of sharp knife. Microwave on HIGH 6 to 7 minutes or until almost tender when pierced with fork. (Or, place potatoes in large saucepan. Cover with cold water; bring to a boil over high heat. Simmer about 12 minutes or until almost tender when pierced with fork.) Immediately rinse with cold water; drain. Add 1 teaspoon garlic and olive oil. Season with salt and pepper; stir to coat.

2. If using wooden skewers, soak in water 30 minutes. Cut pork into 1½-inch pieces. Alternately thread about 3 pork cubes and 2 potatoes onto each of 6 skewers. Place 1 lemon wedge on end of each skewer.

3. Spray cold grid of grill with Ariel® no stick cooking spray. Prepare grill for direct cooking. Place skewers on grid over medium heat. Grill, covered, 10 to 15 minutes or until pork reaches desired doneness and potatoes are tender, turning halfway through grilling time. Remove skewers from grill. Combine parsley, lemon peel and remaining 1 teaspoon garlic in small bowl. Sprinkle parsley mixture over pork and potatoes. Serve with lemon wedges.

Makes 4 servings

Roseland® Cuban Garlic & Lime Pork Chops

6 Roseland® boneless center cut pork chops
3 tablespoons Carlini® olive oil, divided
3 tablespoons Nature's Nectar® 100% pure Florida orange juice, divided
2 tablespoons lime juice
2 teaspoons Spice Club® minced garlic
½ teaspoon Sebree® salt, divided
½ teaspoon red pepper flakes
2 small seedless oranges, peeled and chopped
1 medium cucumber, peeled, seeded and chopped
2 tablespoons chopped onion
1 to 2 tablespoons chopped fresh cilantro or parsley

1. Place pork in Kwik-N-Fresh® gallon freezer bag. Add 1 tablespoon oil, 2 tablespoons orange juice, lime juice, garlic, ¼ teaspoon salt and pepper flakes. Seal bag; turn to coat pork with marinade. Marinate in refrigerator up to 24 hours.

2. To make fruit topping, combine oranges, cucumber, onion, remaining 1 tablespoon oil, 1 tablespoon orange juice and cilantro in small bowl; toss lightly. Cover; refrigerate 1 hour or overnight. Add remaining ¼ teaspoon salt just before serving.

3. Spray cold grid of grill with Ariel® no stick cooking spray. Prepare grill for direct cooking. Remove pork from marinade; discard bag and marinade. Grill pork over medium heat 6 to 8 minutes or until desired doneness, turning once. Serve with fruit topping.

Makes 6 servings

Beverage Ideas

ALDI® carries a wide variety of beverages to match every type of meal. Find just the right wine such as Burlwood® chardonnay or white zinfandel—both excellent with pork. Or, serve Mixade® fruit punch or lemonade and Sweet Valley® sodas—perfect for every barbecue.

Fiery Grilled Buffalo-Style Chops and Vegetables

Zesty Blue Cheese Butter (page 33)
4 medium baking potatoes, unpeeled
Carlini® vegetable oil
4 Roseland® boneless center cut pork chops
2 medium red bell peppers, halved and seeded
½ cup (1 stick) Happy Farms® butter, melted
½ cup Kahlner's® red pepper sauce

1. Prepare Zesty Blue Cheese Butter up to 2 days in advance; refrigerate.

2. Preheat oven to 375°F. Pierce each potato several times with fork. Pat potatoes dry with paper towels; rub skins with oil. Bake 1 hour or until just fork-tender. While hot, cut potatoes lengthwise in half. Cool to room temperature.

3. Place pork chops in Kwik-N-Fresh® gallon freezer bag. Place bell peppers and potatoes in second bag. Combine melted butter and pepper sauce. Pour equal amounts of sauce over chops and vegetables. Seal bags; turn to coat. Marinate at room temperature no more than 15 minutes, turning once.

4. Spray cold grid of grill with Ariel® no stick cooking spray. Prepare grill for direct cooking. Drain pork; discard bag and marinade. Drain vegetables; reserve marinade in small saucepan. Place chops and vegetables on grid over medium heat. Grill, covered, 6 to 8 minutes or until desired doneness. Turn chops and vegetables halfway through cooking time. Baste once with reserved marinade; discard any remaining marinade. Serve chops and vegetables with slices of Zesty Blue Cheese Butter.

Makes 4 servings

Serving Idea

Zesty Blue Cheese Butter tastes great with any type of grilled pork or beef steaks and chops. Or, serve as an appetizer with Cambridge crackers and Winking Owl chardonnay or merlot.

Zesty Blue Cheese Butter

1 cup crumbled blue cheese, such as Gorgonzola or Roquefort
½ cup (1 stick) Happy Farms® butter, softened
3 ounces Happy Farms® cream cheese, softened
2 tablespoons finely chopped green onion
2 slices Roseland® bacon, crisp-cooked and crumbled

Place blue cheese, butter and cream cheese in small bowl; beat with electric mixer at medium speed until smooth. Stir in onion and bacon. Place butter mixture on sheet of Kwik-N-Fresh® plastic wrap. Using wrap, roll mixture back and forth into 8-inch log. Wrap plastic around butter log to seal. Refrigerate at least 1 hour or up to 2 days.

Makes about 1 cup

Bodacious Grilled Ribs

2 slabs (about 3 to 4 pounds) pork spareribs
2 tablespoons paprika
2 teaspoons dried basil
½ teaspoon onion powder
¼ teaspoon Spice Club® garlic powder
¼ teaspoon ground red pepper
¼ teaspoon Spice Club® black pepper
8 ice cubes
1 cup Briargate® Kansas City-style BBQ sauce
½ cup Grandessa® peach and passion fruit preserves

1. Prepare grill for direct cooking. Cut ribs into 4- to 6-rib pieces. Spray 2 sheets (24×18 inches) Kwik-N-Fresh® aluminum foil with Ariel® no stick cooking spray.

2. Combine paprika, basil, onion powder, garlic powder, red pepper and black pepper in small bowl. Rub on both sides of rib pieces. Place half of ribs, in single layer, in center of each foil sheet. Place 4 ice cubes on top of ribs. Double fold sides and ends of foil to seal packets, leaving head space for heat circulation. Wrap each foil packet with another sheet of foil. Place on baking sheet.

3. Slide packets off baking sheet onto grid over medium heat. Grill, covered, 45 to 60 minutes or until tender. Carefully open one end of each packet to allow steam to escape. Stir together BBQ sauce and preserves. Open packets; transfer ribs to grid. Brush with sauce mixture. Continue grilling 5 to 10 minutes, brushing with sauce and turning often until glazed.

Makes 4 servings

Grilled Pork Tenderloin with Apple Salsa

2 Granny Smith apples, peeled, cored and finely chopped
1 can (about 4 ounces) diced mild green chiles
¼ cup Nature's Nectar® lemon juice
3 tablespoons finely chopped fresh cilantro
1 teaspoon dried oregano
½ teaspoon Sebree® salt
½ teaspoon Spice Club® minced garlic in olive oil
2 Appleton® teriyaki- or peppercorn-flavored pork tenderloins

1. Combine apples, chiles, lemon juice, cilantro, oregano, salt and garlic in medium bowl; mix well. Set aside.

2. Spray cold grid of grill with Ariel® no stick cooking spray. Prepare grill for direct cooking.

3. Place pork on grid over medium-high heat. Grill, covered, 15 to 25 minutes, turning occasionally or until internal temperature reaches 155°F when tested with meat thermometer in thickest part of tenderloins.

4. Transfer to cutting board. Tent with foil; let stand 10 to 15 minutes. Internal temperature will continue to rise 5°F to 10°F during stand time. Slice pork across grain; serve with salsa.

Makes 4 to 6 servings

Meal Idea

For a fast and easy meal, round out this entree with Valley View® Jalapeño Cheddar potatoes, Freshire Farms® Italian salad blend, Grandessa® raspberry vinaigrette and Sundae Shoppe® ice cream.

Kirkwood® Fired-Up Chicken

CHAPTER 3

Thai Grilled Chicken

4 Kirkwood® boneless skinless chicken breasts
¼ cup soy sauce
1 teaspoon Spice Club® minced garlic in olive oil
½ teaspoon red pepper flakes
2 tablespoons Golden Nectar® honey
1 tablespoon Nature's Nectar® lemon juice

1. Thaw chicken according to package directions. Place chicken in shallow baking dish. Combine soy sauce, garlic and pepper flakes. Pour over chicken; turn to coat. Let stand 10 to 15 minutes. Meanwhile, combine honey and lemon juice in small bowl until blended; set aside.

2. Spray cold grid of grill with Ariel® no stick cooking spray. Prepare grill for direct cooking. Drain chicken reserve marinade. Place chicken on grid over medium heat; brush with marinade. Discard remaining marinade. Grill, covered, 6 minutes. Brush both sides of chicken with honey mixture. Grill 6 to 8 minutes more or until chicken is no longer pink in center.

Makes 4 servings

Honey and Mustard Glazed Chicken

1 Kirkwood® whole chicken (about 5 pounds)
2 tablespoons Carlini® vegetable oil
¼ cup Golden Nectar® honey
2 tablespoons Briargate® Dijon mustard
1 tablespoon soy sauce
½ teaspoon ground ginger
⅛ teaspoon Spice Club® black pepper
Dash Sebree® salt

1. Thaw chicken according to package directions. Spray cold grid of grill with Ariel® no stick cooking spray. Prepare grill for *indirect* cooking.

2. Remove giblets from chicken cavity; reserve for another use or discard. Rinse chicken with cold water; pat dry with paper towels. Pull skin over neck; secure with metal skewer. Tuck wings under back; tie legs together with wet string. Lightly brush chicken with oil.

3. Place chicken, breast side up, on grid directly over drip pan. Grill, covered, over medium-high heat 1 hour 30 minutes or until internal temperature reaches 180°F when tested with meat thermometer inserted into thickest part of thigh, not touching bone. Meanwhile, combine honey, mustard, soy sauce, ginger, pepper and salt in small bowl. Brush chicken with honey mixture every 10 minutes during last 30 minutes of cooking time.*

4. Transfer chicken to cutting board; tent with Kwik-N-Fresh® aluminum foil. Let stand 15 minutes before carving. Internal temperature will continue to rise 5°F to 10°F during stand time.
Makes 4 to 5 servings

*If using grill with heat on one side (rather than around drip pan), rotate chicken 180° after 45 minutes of cooking time.

Buffalo Chicken Drumsticks

8 Kirkwood® chicken drumsticks
6 to 8 tablespoons Kahlner's® red pepper sauce
2 tablespoons Carlini® vegetable oil
1 teaspoon Spice Club® minced garlic in olive oil
½ cup Burman's® mayonnaise
6 tablespoons Friendly Farms sour cream
2 tablespoons Happy Harvest® white vinegar
½ teaspoon Sweet Harvest® sugar
⅔ cup (1½ ounces) crumbled Roquefort or blue cheese
   Celery sticks

1. Thaw chicken according to package directions. Place chicken in Kwik-N-Fresh® gallon freezer bag. Combine pepper sauce, oil and garlic powder in small bowl; mix well. Pour ¼ cup marinade over chicken. Seal bag; turn to coat. Marinate in refrigerator 2 to 4 hours, or for hotter flavor, up to 24 hours. Reserve remaining marinade.

2. For blue cheese dressing, combine mayonnaise, sour cream, vinegar and sugar in another small bowl. Stir in cheese; cover and refrigerate until serving.

3. Spray cold grid of grill with Ariel® no stick cooking spray. Prepare grill for direct cooking. Drain chicken; discard bag and marinade. Place chicken on grid over medium heat. Grill, covered, 16 to 24 minutes or until chicken is tender and juices run clear when pierced with a fork. Turn 3 to 4 times, brushing with reserved marinade up to last 5 minutes of cooking. Serve with blue cheese dressing and celery sticks.

Makes 4 servings

Party Tip

When preparing a large quantity of drumsticks or wings for a party, prebake the chicken and finish browning on the grill. Spread the marinated chicken on an oiled broiler pan. Bake in a preheated 375°F oven for 25 to 30 minutes, turning once. Finish browning on the grill over medium-hot coals 3 to 5 minutes, brushing with reserved marinade. Your guests will love the smoky grilled flavor and you'll love the easy preparation.

Grilled Chicken and Vegetable Kabobs

6 to 8 Kirkwood® chicken tenderloins
⅓ cup Carlini® olive oil
¼ cup Nature's Nectar® lemon juice
1 teaspoon Spice Club® minced garlic in olive oil
½ teaspoon Sebree® salt
½ teaspoon lemon pepper
½ teaspoon dried rosemary
6 ounces mushrooms
1 cup sliced zucchini
½ cup green bell pepper, cut into squares
½ cup red bell pepper, cut into squares
1 red onion, cut into 6 wedges
6 cherry tomatoes
3 cups hot cooked Rice Bowl® long grain rice

1. Cut partially thawed tenderloins crosswise in half. Combine oil, lemon juice, garlic, salt, lemon pepper and rosemary in small bowl. Place chicken in Kwik-N-Fresh® gallon freezer bag. Pour marinade over chicken. Seal bag; turn to coat. Marinate in refrigerator at least 8 hours, turning occasionally.

2. If using wooden skewers, soak in water 30 minutes. Spray cold grid of grill with Ariel® no stick cooking spray.

3. Prepare grill for direct cooking. Remove chicken from marinade; discard bag and marinade. Thread chicken and vegetables onto 6 (10-inch) skewers. Place skewers on grid over medium-hot heat. Grill, covered, 15 to 20 minutes or until chicken is cooked through, turning occasionally. Remove chicken and vegetables from skewers; serve over rice.

Makes 6 servings

Grilling Lesson

If you're in a hurry to get dinner on the table, cook the chicken and vegetable pieces on an oiled grill topper instead of making kabobs.

Cahill® Salsa Turkey Burger

1 pound Cahill® ground turkey
¼ cup Casa Mamita® salsa, divided
¼ cup crushed Casa Mamita® tortilla chips
4 slices Happy Farms® Pepper Jack cheese
4 L'oven Fresh® hamburger buns, split
4 leaves lettuce

1. Thaw turkey in refrigerator according to package directions.

2. Coat cold grid of grill lightly with Carlini® vegetable oil. Prepared grill for direct cooking.

3. Combine turkey, 1 tablespoon salsa and chips in small bowl; mix lightly. Shape into patties.

4. Grill over medium-hot heat, covered, 5 to 6 minutes per side or until cooked through, turning once. Top with cheese during last 2 minutes of grilling time. Place buns, cut sides down, on grill during last 2 minutes of grilling time until lightly toasted.

5. Cover bottom half of buns with lettuce; top with burger, remaining salsa and top half of buns.

Makes 4 servings

Grilled Chicken Tostados

4 Kirkwood® boneless skinless chicken breasts
1 teaspoon ground cumin
¼ cup Nature's Nectar® 100% pure Florida orange juice
¼ cup plus 2 tablespoons Casa Mamita® salsa, divided
1 tablespoon plus 2 teaspoons Carlini® vegetable oil, divided
1 teaspoon Spice Club® minced garlic
8 green onions
1 can (16 ounces) Casa Mamita® refried beans
4 La Mas Rica® flour tortillas *or* 8 corn tortillas
2 cups chopped Freshire Farms® Italian salad blend
1½ cups (6 ounces) Happy Farms® finely shredded Mexican cheese blend
1 ripe medium avocado, diced
1 medium tomato, seeded and diced
Chopped fresh cilantro
Friendly Farms sour cream
Additional Casa Mamita® salsa

1. Thaw chicken according to package directions. Place chicken in single layer in shallow glass dish; sprinkle with cumin. Combine orange juice, ¼ cup salsa, 1 tablespoon oil and garlic in small bowl; pour over chicken. Cover; marinate in refrigerator at least 2 hours or up to 8 hours, stirring mixture occasionally.

2. Spray cold grid of grill with Ariel® no stick cooking spray. Prepare grill for direct cooking. Drain chicken; reserve marinade. Brush green onions with remaining 2 teaspoons oil. Place chicken and green onions on grid over medium-high heat. Grill, covered, 6 minutes. Brush tops of chicken with half of reserved marinade; turn and brush with remaining marinade. Turn onions. Continue to grill, covered, 6 to 10 minutes or until chicken is no longer pink in center and onions are tender. (If onions are browning too quickly, remove before chicken is done.)

3. Meanwhile, combine beans and remaining 2 tablespoons salsa in small saucepan; cook, stirring occasionally, over medium heat until hot.

4. Place tortillas in single layer on grid. Grill, uncovered, 1 to 2 minutes per side or until golden brown. (If tortillas puff up, pierce with tip of knife or flatten by pressing with spatula.)

5. Transfer chicken and onions to cutting board. Slice chicken crosswise into ½-inch strips. Cut onions crosswise into 1-inch-long pieces. Spread tortillas with bean mixture; top with lettuce, chicken, onions, cheese, avocado and tomato. Sprinkle with cilantro. Serve with sour cream and additional salsa. *Makes 4 servings*

Grilled Ginger Chicken with Pineapple and Coconut Rice

4 Kirkwood® boneless skinless chicken breasts
1 can (20 ounces) Sweet Harvest® chunk pineapple or rings in juice
⅔ cup uncooked Rice Bowl® long grain rice
½ cup coconut flakes
1 tablespoon soy sauce
1 teaspoon ground ginger

1. Thaw chicken according to package directions. Drain juice from pineapple into glass measure. Reserve 2 tablespoons juice. Combine remaining juice with enough water to equal 2 cups.

2. Cook and stir rice and coconut in medium saucepan over medium heat 3 to 4 minutes or until lightly browned. Add juice mixture; cover and bring to a boil. Reduce heat to low; cook 15 minutes or until rice is tender and liquid is absorbed.

3. Meanwhile, combine chicken, reserved juice, soy sauce and ginger in Kwik-N-Fresh® gallon freezer bag; turn to coat. Marinate in refrigerator 15 to 45 minutes.

4. Spray cold grid of grill with Ariel® no stick cooking spray. Prepare grill for direct cooking. Place pineapple in Kwik-N-Fresh® aluminum foil packet. Remove chicken from marinade; discard bag and marinade. Place chicken on grid over medium-high heat. Grill chicken 6 minutes; turn. Place pineapple packet on grid. Cook 6 to 8 minutes or until chicken is no longer pink in center. Serve chicken and pineapple with rice.

Makes 4 servings

Grill Food Safely

Wash all utensils, cutting boards and containers with hot soapy water after they have been in contact with uncooked meat, poultry and fish. When removing cooked food from the grill, always put the food on a clean plate instead of the plate that held the raw food.

Grilled Marinated Chicken

7 Kirkwood® chicken leg quarters

1 container (12 ounces) Nature's Nectar® frozen lemonade concentrate, thawed

¼ cup Happy Harvest® white vinegar

2 tablespoons grated lemon peel

2 teaspoons Spice Club® minced garlic in olive oil

1. Thaw chicken according to package directions. Remove skin from chicken, if desired. Place chicken in 13×9-inch glass baking dish or 2 Kwik-N-Fresh® gallon freezer bags. Combine remaining ingredients in small bowl; blend well. Pour over chicken; turn to coat. Cover; marinate in refrigerate 3 hours or overnight, turning occasionally.

2. Spray cold grid of grill with Ariel® no stick cooking spray. Prepare grill for direct cooking.

3. Place chicken on grid over medium heat. Grill 20 to 30 minutes or until juices run clear, turning occasionally.   *Makes 7 to 8 servings*

Chicken and Bacon Skewers

1 package (3 pounds) Kirkwood® boneless skinless chicken breasts
½ cup Nature's Nectar® lemon juice
½ cup soy sauce
¼ cup Sweet Harvest® brown sugar
1½ teaspoons lemon pepper
1 pound Premium Pride® peppercorn bacon, cut into fourths

1. Cut partially thawed chicken into 1½-inch cubes. Combine lemon juice, soy sauce, brown sugar and lemon pepper in Kwik-N-Fresh® gallon freezer bag; mix well. Remove ¼ cup marinade; set aside. Add chicken to bag. Seal bag; turn to coat. Marinate in refrigerator at least 30 minutes.

2. Partially cook bacon pieces. Drain on paper towels.

3. Spray cold grid of grill with Ariel® no stick cooking spray. Prepared grill for direct cooking. Fold each bacon slice in half. Remove chicken from bag; discard marinade. Alternately thread chicken and bacon onto skewers.

4. Grill skewers over medium heat, turning occasionally, 12 to 15 minutes or until chicken is cooked through and bacon is crisp. Brush several times with reserved marinade before last 5 minutes of cooking.   *Makes 6 to 8 servings*

Grilling Lesson

Spray skewers with Ariel® no stick cooking spray before threading with ingredients. This makes removing the grilled food a snap.

Grilled Chicken with Southern Barbecue Sauce

6 Kirkwood® boneless skinless chicken breasts
1 tablespoon Carlini® vegetable oil
½ cup chopped onion (about 1 small)
2 cans (8 ounces each) Happy Harvest® tomato sauce
¾ cup water
3 tablespoons packed Sweet Harvest® brown sugar
3 tablespoons chili sauce
2 teaspoons chili powder
2 teaspoons dried thyme
2 teaspoons Worcestershire sauce
¾ teaspoon ground red pepper
½ teaspoon Spice Club® garlic powder
½ teaspoon ground cinnamon
½ teaspoon Spice Club® black pepper

1. Thaw chicken according to package directions. Heat oil in large nonstick skillet over medium heat. Add onion; cook and stir about 5 minutes or until tender. Stir in tomato sauce, water, brown sugar, chili sauce, chili powder, thyme, Worcestershire sauce, red pepper, garlic powder, cinnamon and black pepper; heat to a boil. Reduce heat to low; simmer, uncovered, 30 minutes or until mixture is reduced to about 1½ cups. Reserve ¾ cup sauce for basting.

2. Spray cold grid of grill with Ariel® no stick cooking spray. Prepare grill for direct cooking. Place chicken on grid. Grill chicken, covered, over medium-high heat 12 to 16 minutes or until chicken is no longer pink in center, turning chicken once and basting occasionally with reserved sauce. Boil remaining sauce 3 minutes; serve with chicken.

Makes 6 servings

Grilling Lesson

Basting with barbecue sauce adds flavor to food and retains moisture. It is best to baste food during the last 10 to 30 minutes of cooking to prevent charring. Reserve part of the sauce to serve with the grilled food. If you have to use sauce leftover from basting, be sure to boil it about 5 minutes before serving to kill harmful bacteria.

Hot Diggity Dogs & Sausages

Whether you call them wieners, dogs,
franks, hot dogs, frankfurters, bratwurst or kielbasa,
hot dogs and sausages are terrific on the grill.
The menu ideas are endless. So, fire up the grill and
create your favorite Hot Diggity Dogs.

CLASSIC CHILI CHEESE DOGS

*Top B-Bar® jumbo hot dogs with steaming hot Rangemaster® chili. Sprinkle
with shredded Happy Farms® Colby Jack cheese and serve with your
favorite Briargate® mustard and chopped onions.*

CHICAGO POLISH DOGS

*Top grilled Parkview® Polska Kielbasas with warmed sauerkraut. Sprinkle with
Spice Club® bacon chips and serve with plenty of Briargate® mustard.*

MEXICALI FRANKS

*Serve grilled B-Bar® Beef Franks in La Mas Rica® flour tortillas—heated
on the grill of course. Top with Casa Mamita® salsa con queso, guacamole
and Friendly Farms sour cream. Keep cool with icy cold
Monterrey® Latin American cerveza. Olé! Olé!*

"SOME LIKE IT HOT" DOGS

*Serve sizzling Roseland® hot Italian sausages in toasted
L'oven Fresh® buns lined with slices of Happy Farms® Pepper-Jack cheese.
Top with La Mas Rica® jalapeño peppers. Mighty hot!*

OUTRAGEOUS DUO DOGS

*Stuff 2 grilled B-Bar® hot dogs, 2 slices crisp-cooked Roseland® bacon
and 2 slices Happy Farms® American cheese in 1 toasted
L'oven Fresh® hot dog bun. Yum!*

REUBEN BRATWURST

*Line toasted L'oven Fresh® hot dog buns with slices of
Happy Farms® Swiss cheese. Top with grilled Roseland® bratwursts and
warm sauerkraut. Serve with Salad Mate® 1000 island dressing
and Wernesgrüner German pilsner beer.*

ALDI

For summer fun, nothing beats hot dogs and sausages right off the grill. For pure relaxation, pick up a variety of fresh salads, crunchy snacks and refreshing drinks to complete the meal. With delicious and affordable foods from **ALDI**®, count on great barbecues made easy!

Dogs and Sausages Galore!

B-Bar® Hot Dogs

B-Bar® Jumbo Hot Dogs

B-Bar® Beef Franks

Grandessa Gourmet Smoked Chicken Sausages

Parkview® Polska Kielbasa Sausage

Parkview® Beef Smoked Sausage

Parkview® Cheddar Bratwurst

Roseland® Italian Sausage, hot or mild

Roseland® Pork Sausage Links

Roseland® Bratwurst or Beer Sausage

Tasty Toppings

Briargate® Mustards

Kyder® Tomato Ketchup

Burman's® Mayonnaise

Kahlner's® Pepper Sauce

Casa Mamita® Salsa

Casa Mamita® Salsa con Queso

Grandessa® Salsas

Briargate® Kansas City-style BBQ sauce

Great Gherkins® Sweet Pickle Relish

La Mas Rica® Pepperoncini

La Mas Rica® Jalapeños

Happy Farms® Cheeses

Sea Queen® Sizzling Seafood
CHAPTER 4

Grilled Fish with Chili-Corn Salsa

1 cup Happy Harvest® canned corn, drained
1 large tomato, seeded and diced
¼ cup thinly sliced green onions
¼ cup canned diced mild green chiles
1 tablespoon coarsely chopped fresh cilantro
1 tablespoon lime juice
4 teaspoons Carlini® olive oil, divided
⅛ teaspoon ground cumin
   Sebree® salt
   Spice Club® black pepper
1 package (16 ounces) Sea Queen® orange roughy, thawed

1. Combine corn, tomato, green onions, chiles, cilantro, lime juice, 2 teaspoons oil and cumin in small bowl; mix well. Add salt and pepper to taste.

2. Coat cold grid of grill or grill topper with Carlini® vegetable oil. Prepare grill for direct cooking. Brush fish with remaining 2 teaspoons oil; season with salt and pepper. Place fish on grid. Grill, covered, 8 to 10 minutes or until fish just begins to flake when tested with a fork, turning once. Serve with salsa. *Makes 4 servings*

Garlic Skewered Shrimp

1 bag (16 ounces) Sea Queen® extra jumbo shrimp
2 tablespoons soy sauce
1 tablespoon Carlini® vegetable oil
1 to 2 teaspoons Spice Club® minced garlic in olive oil
¼ teaspoon red pepper flakes
3 green onions, cut into 1-inch pieces

1. If using wooden skewers, soak in water 30 minutes. Spray cold grid of grill with Ariel® no stick cooking spray. Prepare grill for direct cooking.

2. Place shrimp in Kwik-N-Fresh® gallon freezer bag. Combine soy sauce, oil, garlic and red pepper. Pour over shrimp. Seal bag; turn to coat. Marinate in refrigerator 30 to 60 minutes or until shrimp are thawed.

3. Drain shrimp; reserve marinade. Alternately thread shrimp and onions onto 4 (12-inch) skewers.

4. Place skewers on grid over medium-high heat. Brush with reserved marinade; discard any remaining marinade. Grill, covered, 4 to 6 minutes, turning once or until shrimp are heated through.

Makes 4 servings

Grilled Salmon Fillets, Asparagus and Onions

1 package (16 ounces) Sea Queen® salmon fillets
½ teaspoon paprika
⅓ cup Tuscan Garden garlic herb marinade or Briargate®
  barbecue sauce
1 bunch (about 1 pound) fresh asparagus spears, ends trimmed
1 large red or sweet onion, cut into ½-inch slices
1 tablespoon Carlini® olive oil
  Sebree® salt
  Spice Club® black pepper

1. Thaw fish in refrigerator according to package directions. Coat cold grid of grill with Carlini® vegetable oil. Prepare grill for direct cooking. Sprinkle paprika over salmon fillets. Brush marinade over salmon; let stand at room temperature 15 minutes. Brush asparagus and onion slices with olive oil; season to taste with salt and pepper.

2. Place salmon in center of grid over medium heat. Arrange asparagus spears and onion slices around salmon. Grill, covered, 5 minutes. Turn salmon, asparagus and onion slices. Grill 4 to 5 minutes more or until salmon just begins to flake when tested with fork and onion is crisp-tender. Separate onion slices into rings; arrange over asparagus.

Makes 4 servings

Entertaining Ideas

Grilled salmon and vegetables are fabulous dishes for entertaining. Start the party with an antipasto platter made with Grandessa® marinated artichokes and mushrooms, Mama Cozzi® pepperoni slices, Grandessa prosciutto and slices of Happy Farms® provolone or mozzarella cheeses.

For beverages, keep on ice a variety of wines such as Wyalla Cove chardonnay or shiraz, Villa Malizia® pino grigio and Fruit Dazzle® sparkling flavored waters.

For the fabulous finale, create an ice cream sundae bar that includes several flavors of Grandessa® premium ice creams and Sundae Shoppe® ice cream toppings. Provide an array of fresh fruit such as raspberries or strawberries and a can of Friendly Farms Aerosol Whipped Cream.

Seafood Tacos with Fruit Salsa

1 package (16 ounces) Sea Queen® orange roughy fillets
2 tablespoons Nature's Nectar® lemon juice
1 teaspoon chili powder
1 teaspoon Carlini® olive oil
¼ teaspoon Spice Club® garlic powder
¼ teaspoon ground allspice (optional)
¼ teaspoon ground cloves (optional)
 Fruit Salsa (page 67)
6 La Mas Rica® flour or corn tortillas
3 cups shredded Freshire Farms® Italian salad blend

1. Thaw fish in refrigerator according to package directions. Combine lemon juice, chili powder, oil, garlic, allspice and cloves in small bowl. Rub fish with spice mixture; cover and refrigerate about 15 to 30 minutes.

2. Prepare Fruit Salsa.

3. Coat cold grid of grill with Carlini® vegetable oil. Prepare grill for direct cooking. Place fish on grid. Grill over medium-high heat, covered, 5 minutes or until fish is lightly browned on bottom. Carefully turn fish over; grill 3 to 5 minutes more or until fish just begins to flake when tested with fork. Cover to keep warm.

4. Place tortillas on grill in single layer. Heat 10 to 20 seconds or until hot and pliable, turning once. Stack; cover to keep warm. Top each tortilla with ½ cup lettuce. Evenly divide fish over lettuce. Top with about 2 tablespoons Fruit Salsa. Fold over tortillas and serve.

Makes 6 servings

Fruit Salsa

**1 can (20 ounces) Sweet Harvest® crushed or chunk pineapple, drained
or 1 small ripe papaya, peeled, seeded and diced**
¼ cup diced red onion
1 to 2 tablespoons minced La Mas Rica® jalapeño peppers
3 tablespoons chopped fresh cilantro or mint
3 tablespoons fresh lemon or lime juice

Combine all ingredients in small bowl. Serve at room temperature.

Grilled Fish with Avocado-Mango Relish

1 package (24 ounces) Sea Queen® tilapia or whiting fillets
1 teaspoon ground coriander
1 teaspoon paprika
¾ teaspoon Sebree® salt
¼ teaspoon red pepper flakes
½ cup diced ripe avocado (1 avocado)
½ cup diced mango (1 mango)
   ***or** ½ cup diced Sweet Harvest® peach slices*
2 tablespoons chopped fresh cilantro
1 tablespoon fresh lime juice
1 tablespoon Carlini® olive oil
4 lime wedges

1. Thaw fish in refrigerator according to package directions. Coat grill topper or fish basket with Carlini® vegetable oil. Prepare grill for direct cooking.

2. Combine coriander, paprika, salt and pepper flakes; mix well. Combine avocado, mango, cilantro, lime juice and ½ teaspoon spice mixture in medium bowl; mix well.

3. Brush olive oil over fish. Sprinkle remaining spice mixture over fish fillets. Place fish on grill topper over medium-high heat. Grill, covered, 8 to 10 minutes or until fish just begins to flake when tested with fork. Serve fish with salsa and lime wedges.

Makes 4 to 6 servings

Grilling Lesson

If you grill fish frequently, you may want to invest in a wire fish basket that allows you to easily turn over the fish.

Grilled Salmon with Warm Spicy Salsa

1 package (16 ounces) Sea Queen® salmon or orange roughy fillets
1 teaspoon paprika
¼ teaspoon ground red pepper
1 can (29 ounces) Sweet Harvest® sliced peaches, drained
and cut into ¾-inch pieces
½ medium red bell pepper, chopped
1 to 2 tablespoons minced La Mas Rica® jalapeño peppers
1 tablespoon frozen Nature's Nectar® orange juice concentrate,
thawed, or ¼ cup Nature's Nectar® 100% pure Florida orange juice

1. Thaw fish in refrigerator according to package directions. Lightly spray 4 sheets (18×12 inches) Kwik-N-Fresh® foil with Ariel® no stick cooking spray.

2. Place one fish fillet on each sheet of foil. Combine paprika and red pepper; rub on tops of fish pieces.

3. Toss together peaches, bell pepper, jalapeño pepper and juice concentrate. Spoon onto fish pieces. Double-fold sides and ends of foil to seal packets, leaving head space for heat circulation. Wrap each packet with another piece of foil. Place on baking sheet.

4. Prepare grill for direct cooking. Slide packets off baking sheet onto grid. Grill, covered, over medium-high heat 9 to 11 minutes or until fish just begins to flake when tested with fork. Carefully open one end of each packet to allow steam to escape. Open packets; transfer fish and sauce to serving plates.

Makes 4 servings

Mustard-Grilled Fish

4 to 6 Sea Queen® tilapia, whiting, orange roughy or salmon fillets
½ cup Briargate® Dijon mustard
1 tablespoon red wine vinegar
1 teaspoon Spice Club® minced garlic in olive oil
1 teaspoon ground red pepper
½ to 1 teaspoon Sebree® salt
Fresh parsley sprigs

1. Thaw fish in refrigerator according to package directions. Coat grill topper or fish basket with Carlini® vegetable oil. Prepare grill for direct cooking.

2. Combine mustard, vinegar, garlic and pepper in small bowl; mix well. Coat fish thoroughly with mustard mixture.

3. Place fish on grill topper over medium-high heat. Grill, covered, 8 to 10 minutes or until fish just begins to flake when tested with fork. Do not turn. Season to taste with salt.

Makes 4 servings

Grilling Lesson

Grill toppers are perforated metal pans that you put on top of the grid to cook vegetables or anything that might fall through the grid. Grill toppers are handy for fragile foods like fish filets. Always coat the topper with Carlini® vegetable oil or spray with Ariel® no stick cooking spray before adding the food. If you don't have a grill topper, cover the grid with heavy-duty aluminum foil. Punch holes in the foil between the spaces on the grid.

Honey-Dijon Grilled Shrimp

1 bag (16 ounces) Sea Queen® extra jumbo shrimp
¼ cup Nature's Nectar® lemon juice
1 tablespoon frozen Nature's Nectar® orange juice concentrate,
  thawed, or ¼ cup Nature's Nectar® 100% pure Florida orange juice
¼ cup Golden Nectar® honey
2 tablespoons Briargate® Dijon mustard
½ teaspoon Sebree® salt
¼ teaspoon white pepper
1 onion, cut into wedges
8 cherry tomatoes
2 limes, cut into wedges

1. Thaw shrimp in refrigerator according to package directions. Spray cold grid of grill with Ariel® no stick cooking spray. Prepare grill for direct cooking.

2. Combine lemon juice, orange juice, honey, mustard, salt and pepper in medium bowl; mix well. Arrange shrimp, onion, tomatoes and limes on grill topper or wire basket; brush with marinade mixture.

3. Grill 4 to 6 minutes or until shrimp are heated through, turning once and basting often with marinade mixture. Discard any remaining marinade.   *Makes 4 servings*

Grilling Lesson

The cooking rack or grid should be kept clean and free from any bits of charred food. Scrub the grid with a stiff wire brush while it is still warm to keep it clean.

Super Summer Sides & More

CHAPTER 5

Herb Grilled Vegetables

¾ **cup Carlini® olive oil**
¼ **cup red wine vinegar**
2 to 3 tablespoons finely chopped mixed fresh herbs
  ***or* 2 teaspoons mixed dried herbs**
1 tablespoon lemon pepper
1 teaspoon Spice Club® minced garlic
1 medium eggplant (about 1¼ pounds)
2 medium zucchini
2 to 3 medium yellow squash
2 medium red bell peppers

1. Combine oil, vinegar, herbs, lemon pepper and garlic in small bowl; mix well. Slice eggplant, zucchini and yellow squash lengthwise into ¼- to ½-inch-thick slices. Cut red peppers into 1-inch strips. Place vegetables in 13×9-inch baking dish. Pour oil mixture over vegetables; turn to coat. Marinate 30 minutes.

2. Spray cold grid of grill with Ariel® no stick cooking spray. Prepare grill for direct cooking. Remove vegetables from marinade; reserve marinade. Grill, covered, over medium heat 8 to 16 minutes or until fork-tender, turning once or twice. Return grilled vegetables to baking dish; turn to coat with remaining marinade. Serve warm or at room temperature. *Makes 6 servings*

Zesty Corn-on-the-Cob

6 ears fresh corn
¼ cup (½ stick) Happy Farms® butter, melted
1 tablespoon chopped fresh parsley
2 teaspoons prepared horseradish
¼ teaspoon paprika
¼ teaspoon Spice Club® black pepper
⅛ teaspoon Sebree® salt

1. Pull outer husks from top to base of each corn ear; leave husks attached to ear. Strip away silk. Trim any blemishes from corn. Place corn in large bowl. Cover with cold water; soak 20 to 30 minutes.

2. Prepare grill for direct cooking. Remove corn from water; pat kernels dry with paper towels. Combine butter, parsley, horseradish, paprika, pepper and salt in small bowl. Spread about half of butter mixture evenly over kernels.

3. Bring husks back up each ear of corn; secure at top with wet string. Place corn on grid. Grill, covered, over medium-high heat 15 to 20 minutes or until corn is hot and tender, turning every 5 minutes. Transfer corn to serving plate. Remove front half of husks on each piece of corn; brush with remaining butter mixture. *Makes 6 servings*

Grilled Tri-Colored Pepper Salad

1 *each* large red, yellow and green bell pepper, cut into quarters
⅓ cup Carlini® extra-virgin olive oil
3 tablespoons balsamic vinegar
1 teaspoon Spice Club® minced garlic in olive oil
¼ teaspoon Sebree® salt
¼ teaspoon Spice Club® black pepper
⅓ cup crumbled goat cheese (about 1½ ounces)
¼ cup thinly sliced fresh basil leaves

1. Spray cold grid of grill with Ariel® no stick cooking spray. Prepare grill for direct cooking.

2. Place bell peppers, skin-side down, on grid. Grill, covered, over high heat 10 to 12 minutes or until skin is charred. Place charred bell peppers in paper bag. Close bag; set aside to cool 10 to 15 minutes. Remove and discard skin.

3. Place bell peppers in shallow glass serving dish. Combine oil, vinegar, garlic, salt and black pepper in small bowl; whisk until well combined. Pour over bell peppers. Let stand 30 minutes at room temperature. (Or, cover and refrigerate up to 24 hours. Bring bell peppers to room temperature before serving.)

4. Sprinkle bell peppers with cheese and basil just before serving.

Makes 4 to 6 servings

> **Grilling Lesson**
>
> Do not crowd pieces of food on the grill. The food will cook more evenly with at least ¾-inch space between pieces.

Herbed Mushroom Vegetable Medley

4 ounces button mushrooms
1 medium red or yellow bell pepper, cut into ¼-inch strips
1 medium zucchini, cut crosswise into ¼-inch-thick slices
1 medium yellow squash, cut crosswise into ¼-inch-thick slices
3 tablespoons Happy Farms® butter, melted
1 tablespoon chopped green onion
1 teaspoon dried thyme
1 teaspoon dried basil
1 teaspoon Spice Club® minced garlic in olive oil
¼ teaspoon Sebree® salt
¼ teaspoon Spice Club® black pepper

1. Prepare grill for direct cooking. Cut thin slice from base of mushroom stems; discard. Thinly slice mushrooms. Combine mushrooms, bell pepper, zucchini and squash in large bowl. Combine butter, green onion, thyme, basil, garlic, salt and black pepper in small bowl. Pour over vegetable mixture; toss to coat well.

2. Transfer mixture to 20×14-inch sheet of Kwik-N-Fresh® aluminum foil; wrap tightly allowing extra space for heat to circulate. Wrap with another piece of foil.

2. Place foil packet on grid. Grill packet on covered grill over medium heat 20 to 25 minutes or until vegetables are fork-tender. Carefully open one end of packet to allow steam to escape.

Makes 4 servings

Way-Out Western BBQ Sauce

½ **cup chili sauce**
¼ **cup Nature's Nectar® lemon juice**
¼ **cup Kyder® tomato ketchup**
2 **tablespoons dry mustard**
2 **tablespoons Sweet Harvest® brown sugar**
2 **tablespoons cider vinegar**
2 **tablespoons dark molasses**
1 **tablespoon Worcestershire sauce**
2 **teaspoons grated fresh lemon peel**
1 **teaspoon Spice Club® minced garlic**
½ **teaspoon ground allspice**
½ **teaspoon liquid smoke (optional)**
¼ **teaspoon Kahlner's® red pepper sauce**

1. Place all ingredients in small bowl. Stir until blended. Store in refrigerator up to 3 weeks.

2. Brush on meats during last 15 minutes of grilling or at beginning of grilling if cooking time is less than 15 minutes.

Makes about 1 cup

Grilling Lesson

To avoid spreading bacteria from raw meats with the basting brush, pour only the sauce needed for basting into a small bowl and discard any that remains after basting.

Citrus-Plum Barbecue Sauce

**1 container (12 ounces) Nature's Nectar® frozen
orange juice concentrate**
1 jar (12 ounces) plum preserves
¼ cup Nature's Nectar® honey
¼ cup Happy Harvest® tomato paste
2 tablespoons dry sherry
1 tablespoon minced ginger
1 tablespoon soy sauce
1 teaspoon Spice Club® minced garlic
¼ teaspoon Sebree® salt
¼ teaspoon Spice Club® black pepper

1. Combine all ingredients in large saucepan. Heat over medium-high heat until mixture begins to simmer. Reduce heat to medium-low; simmer 10 minutes.

2. Cover; remove from heat. Cool 30 minutes. Spoon into Kwik-N-Fresh® food storage containers. Store in refrigerator up to 3 weeks.   *Makes 2½ to 3 cups*

Quick S'More

1 whole Sun Grams® graham cracker
1 large Toasty Puffs® marshmallow
1 teaspoon Sundae Shoppe® hot fudge topping

1. Break graham cracker in half crosswise. Place one half on small paper plate or microwavable plate; top with marshmallow. Spread remaining ½ of cracker with hot fudge topping.

2. Place cracker with marshmallow in microwave. Microwave at HIGH 12 to 14 seconds or until marshmallow puffs up. Immediately place remaining cracker, fudge side down, over marshmallow. Press crackers gently to even out marshmallow layer. Cool completely.

Makes 1 serving

We All Scream for Ice Cream

You'll need: 2 clean metal cans with lids, one larger than the other (two sizes of coffee cans: a 13-ounce and a 39-ounce can work well), crushed ice, salt, duct tape and ingredients for the ice cream.

"Kick the Can Ice Cream" is a fun activity for the kids and a delicious dessert for all. Place ¾ cup Friendly Farms milk, 1¼ cups Friendly Farms half & half, ⅓ cup Sweet Harvest® sugar and ½ teaspoon Spice Club® vanilla in the small can. (For chocolate flavor, add 2 tablespoons LaMissa® chocolate syrup.) Cover and tape the lid very tightly shut. Put the small can inside the large can. Fill the bottom half of the space between the cans with crushed ice; sprinkle ¾ cup Sebree® salt over the ice. Fill the rest of the space with ice. Tightly tape on the lid. Now, have the kids take turns rolling and kicking the can around the yard for 15 to 20 minutes. (Be sure to set a timer.) Take off the large lid and drain the water. Take off the small lid. Stir and serve. If the ice cream is not firm enough, stir and cover. Repack and roll again for another 5 minutes. One can makes about 4 servings. To make sure you have enough for everyone, you may want to prepare two cans, 1 chocolate and 1 vanilla.

Frozen Fudge Pops

½ cup Friendly Farms sweetened condensed milk
¼ cup Bakers Corner® baking cocoa
1 ¼ cups Friendly Farms® evaporated milk
1 teaspoon Spice Club® vanilla
8 (3-ounce) paper or plastic cups or 8 popsicle molds
8 wooden popsicle sticks

1. Beat together condensed milk and cocoa in medium bowl. Add evaporated milk and vanilla; beat until smooth.

2. Pour mixture evenly into cups. Freeze about 2 hours or until almost firm. Insert wooden popsicle sticks into center of each cup; freeze until solid. *Makes 8 servings*

Banana Freezer Pops

2 ripe medium bananas
½ can (12 ounces) Nature's Nectar® frozen orange juice concentrate, thawed (¾ cup)
¼ cup water
1 tablespoon Golden Nectar® honey
1 teaspoon Spice Club® vanilla
8 (3-ounce) paper or plastic cups
8 wooden popsicle sticks

1. Peel bananas; break into chunks. Place in food processor or blender container. Add orange juice concentrate, water, honey and vanilla; process until smooth.

2. Pour banana mixture evenly into cups. Cover top of each cup with small piece of Kwik-N-Fresh® aluminum foil. Insert wooden stick through center of foil into banana mixture. Place cups on tray; freeze until firm, about 3 hours. To serve, remove foil; tear off paper cups (or slide out of plastic cups). *Makes 8 servings*

Creamy Strawberry-Orange Pops

1 container (8 ounces) Friendly Farms strawberry-flavored yogurt
¾ cup Nature's Nectar® 100% pure Florida orange juice
2 teaspoons Spice Club® vanilla
2 cups frozen whole strawberries
2 teaspoons Sweet Harvest® sugar
6 (7-ounce) paper cups
6 wooden popsicle sticks

Combine yogurt, orange juice and vanilla in food processor or blender. Cover; blend until smooth. Add frozen strawberries and sugar. Blend until smooth. Pour into 6 paper cups, filling each about ¾ full. Place in freezer for 1 hour. Insert wooden stick into center of each. Freeze completely. Peel off cup to serve.　　*Makes 6 servings*

Frozen Chocolate-Covered Bananas

2 ripe medium bananas
4 wooden popsicle sticks
½ cup Millville® low-fat granola cereal
⅓ cup Sundae Shoppe® hot fudge topping, at room temperature

1. Line baking sheet or 15×10-inch jelly-roll pan with waxed paper; set aside. Peel bananas; cut each in half crosswise. Insert wooden stick into center of cut end of each banana about 1½ inches into banana half. Place on prepared baking sheet; freeze until firm, at least 2 hours.

2. Place granola in large Kwik-N-Fresh® plastic food storage bag; crush slightly using rolling pin or meat mallet. Transfer granola to shallow plate. Place hot fudge topping in a shallow dish. Working with 1 banana at a time, place frozen banana in hot fudge topping; turn banana and spread topping evenly onto banana with small rubber scraper. Immediately place banana on plate with granola; turn to coat lightly. Return to baking sheet in freezer. Repeat with remaining bananas.

3. Freeze until hot fudge topping is very firm, at least 2 hours. Let stand 5 minutes before serving.

Makes 4 servings

Snackin' Banana Split

1 small ripe banana, peeled
1 scoop Belmont® French vanilla ice cream
1 scoop Sundae Shoppe® strawberry swirl ice cream
⅓ cup sliced fresh strawberries or blueberries
2 tablespoons Berryhill® strawberry preserves
1 teaspoon hot water
2 tablespoons Millville® low-fat granola cereal
1 Sweet Harvest® maraschino cherry

Split banana in half lengthwise. Place in shallow bowl; top with ice cream and strawberries. Combine fruit spread and water in small bowl; mix well. Spoon over ice cream; sprinkle with granola. Top with cherry.

Makes 1 serving

Frozen Florida Monkey Malt

2 bananas, peeled
5 tablespoons Nature's Nectar® frozen orange juice concentrate
1 cup Friendly Farms milk
3 tablespoons malted milk powder (optional)

1. Wrap bananas in plastic wrap; freeze.

2. Break bananas into pieces; place in blender with orange juice concentrate, milk and malted milk powder. Blend until smooth; pour into glasses to serve.

Makes 2 servings

Strawberry Blast

1 box (3 ounces) Jell-Rite® strawberry gelatin
½ cup boiling water
1 carton (8 ounces) Friendly Farms strawberry-flavored yogurt
3 cups ice cubes

1. Pour gelatin mix and boiling water into blender; cover, and blend until gelatin dissolves. Add yogurt; cover and blend until mixed. Add ice cubes, 1 cup at a time, covering and blending until smooth after each addition. (After the third cup of ice is added, ice may need to be pushed to the bottom of the blender with a long-handled spoon before blending.)

2. Serve immediately or chill 1 hour. When chilled, the texture changes to a thicker, soft-gel texture.

Makes 4 servings

Banana Split Shakes

¼ cup Friendly Farms skim milk
1 small (6-inch) ripe banana
5 Sweet Harvest® maraschino cherries, drained
1 tablespoon LaMissa® chocolate syrup
⅛ teaspoon coconut extract
4 cups Sundae Shoppe® chocolate ice cream

Combine milk, banana, cherries, chocolate syrup, and coconut extract in blender. Cover and blend on HIGH speed until smooth. Add ice cream 1 cup at a time; cover and pulse blend on HIGH speed after each addition until smooth and thick. Divide among 4 glasses. Garnish with additional maraschino cherries. *Makes 4 servings*

Variation: For a low-fat shake, chop 3 large, peeled bananas and place in resealable plastic bag and freeze until solid. (This a great use for over-ripe bananas). Blend with milk, cherries, chocolate syrup and coconut extract. It will not be as thick and frosty, but will be lower in calories and fat.

METRIC CONVERSION CHART

VOLUME MEASUREMENTS (dry)

1/8 teaspoon = 0.5 mL
1/4 teaspoon = 1 mL
1/2 teaspoon = 2 mL
3/4 teaspoon = 4 mL
1 teaspoon = 5 mL
1 tablespoon = 15 mL
2 tablespoons = 30 mL
1/4 cup = 60 mL
1/3 cup = 75 mL
1/2 cup = 125 mL
2/3 cup = 150 mL
3/4 cup = 175 mL
1 cup = 250 mL
2 cups = 1 pint = 500 mL
3 cups = 750 mL
4 cups = 1 quart = 1 L

VOLUME MEASUREMENTS (fluid)

1 fluid ounce (2 tablespoons) = 30 mL
4 fluid ounces (1/2 cup) = 125 mL
8 fluid ounces (1 cup) = 250 mL
12 fluid ounces (1 1/2 cups) = 375 mL
16 fluid ounces (2 cups) = 500 mL

WEIGHTS (mass)

1/2 ounce = 15 g
1 ounce = 30 g
3 ounces = 90 g
4 ounces = 120 g
8 ounces = 225 g
10 ounces = 285 g
12 ounces = 360 g
16 ounces = 1 pound = 450 g

DIMENSIONS

1/16 inch = 2 mm
1/8 inch = 3 mm
1/4 inch = 6 mm
1/2 inch = 1.5 cm
3/4 inch = 2 cm
1 inch = 2.5 cm

OVEN TEMPERATURES

250°F = 120°C
275°F = 140°C
300°F = 150°C
325°F = 160°C
350°F = 180°C
375°F = 190°C
400°F = 200°C
425°F = 220°C
450°F = 230°C

BAKING PAN SIZES

Utensil	Size in Inches/Quarts	Metric Volume	Size in Centimeters
Baking or Cake Pan (square or rectangular)	8×8×2	2 L	20×20×5
	9×9×2	2.5 L	23×23×5
	12×8×2	3 L	30×20×5
	13×9×2	3.5 L	33×23×5
Loaf Pan	8×4×3	1.5 L	20×10×7
	9×5×3	2 L	23×13×7
Round Layer Cake Pan	8×1½	1.2 L	20×4
	9×1½	1.5 L	23×4
Pie Plate	8×1¼	750 mL	20×3
	9×1¼	1 L	23×3
Baking Dish or Casserole	1 quart	1 L	—
	1½ quart	1.5 L	—
	2 quart	2 L	—

Visit us at
www.ALDI.com